# Contents

Words appearing in bold, **like this**, are explained in the Glossary

# Elements and atomic structure

We are all surrounded by different substances. If you look around, you will see metals, plastics, water and lots of other solids and liquids. You cannot see the gases in the air, but you know they are there, and there are many other kinds of gases too. So just how many different substances are there? Incredibly, more than 19 million different substances have been discovered, named and catalogued. Around 4000 substances are added to the list each day, yet all of these substances are made from just a few simple substances called **elements**.

## Elements

There are 92 naturally occurring elements and a few **artificial** ones. Elements are substances that cannot be broken down into simpler substances using chemical **reactions**. About three-quarters of the elements are metals, such as titanium and tungsten, and most of the rest are non-metals, such as carbon and oxygen. Some elements, like germanium, are called metalloids because they have some of the properties of metals and some of the properties of non-metals.

## Compounds

Elements can join together in chemical reactions to make **compounds**. For example, iron and oxygen react together to make titanium oxide, and carbon and oxygen react together to make carbon dioxide. This means that nearly all of the millions of different substances in the world are compounds, made up of two or more elements chemically joined together.

*Everything in this busy market in Thailand is made from some of the millions of known chemicals. The boats, river water and food are all made from chemicals – and so are the people!*

# The Transition Metals 1

## Tungsten, Titanium and Other Elements

## Nigel Saunders

Heinemann

**www.heinemann.co.uk/library**
Visit our website to find out more information about Heinemann Library books.

To order:
 Phone 44 (0) 1865 888066
 Send a fax to 44 (0) 1865 314091
 Visit the Heinemann Bookshop at www.heinemann.co.uk/library to browse our catalogue and order online.

First published in Great Britain by Heinemann Library, Halley Court, Jordan Hill, Oxford OX2 8EJ, part of Harcourt Education.
Heinemann is a registered trademark of Harcourt Education Ltd.

© Harcourt Education Ltd 2003
First published in paperback in 2004
The moral right of the proprietor has been asserted.

Editorial: Sarah Eason and Kathy Peltan
Design: David Poole and
    Tinstar Design Limited (www.tinstar.co.uk)
Illustrations: Geoff Ward and Paul Fellows
Picture Research: Rosie Garai
Production: Viv Hichens
Originated by Blenheim Colour Ltd
Printed and bound in Hong Kong and China
    by South China

ISBN 0 431 16985 3  (hardback)
07 06 05 04 03
10 9 8 7 6 5 4 3 2 1

ISBN 0 431 16992 6  (paperback)
08 07 06 05 04
10 9 8 7 6 5 4 3 2 1

**British Library Cataloguing in Publication Data**
Saunders, Nigel
    The transition metals: Tungsten, titanium and other elements. (The periodic table)
    546.6
A full catalogue record for this book is available from the British Library.

**Acknowledgements**
The publishers would like to thank the following for permission to reproduce photographs:
Corbis pp12, 19 (Robert Patrick), 23, 25, 26, 37 (Richard Cummins), 38 (Michael Freeman), 39, 45 (Craig Aurness), 48 (Peter Johnson); Empics p43; Geoscience pp44, 51, 52; Getty Images pp4 (David Noton), 35 (John Lamb) 49 (V.C.L.); NASA p29; Science Photo Library pp14 (David Parker), 15 (Lawrence Berkeley), 28 (Russ Lappa), 33 (Mehau Kulyk MEHAU), 34 (Roberto de Guglielmo), 36 (Charles D Winters), 40 (E R Degginger), 46 (Chris Knapton), 50 (George Lepp), 55 (Kaj R Svensson); Trevor Clifford p31; Tudor Photography p20; Wilson Sporting Goods Company p17.

Cover photograph of the gold bars and nuggets reproduced with permission of Getty Images.

The author would like to thank Angela, Kathryn, David and Jean for all their help and support.

The publishers would like to thank Alexandra Clayton for all her help and support.

Every effort has been made to contact copyright holders of any material reproduced in this book. Any omissions will be rectified in subsequent printings if notice is given to the publishers.

## Atoms

Every substance is made up of tiny particles called **atoms**. An element is made up of just one type of atom, and a compound is made up of two or more types of atom joined together. Atoms are far too small to see, even with a light microscope. Three million scandium atoms stacked on top of each other would make a pile only one millimetre high.

Atoms themselves are made up of even tinier particles called **protons**, **neutrons** and **electrons**. At the centre of each atom there is a **nucleus** made up of protons and neutrons. The electrons are arranged in different energy levels, or shells, around the nucleus. Most of an atom is actually empty space – if an atom were blown up to the same size as an Olympic running track, its nucleus would be about the size of a pea! The electrons, and how they are arranged, are responsible for the ways in which each element can react.

## Elements and groups

Different elements react with other substances in different ways. When scientists first began to study chemical reactions this made it difficult for them to make sense of the reaction they observed. In 1869, a Russian chemist called Dimitri Mendeleev put each element into one of eight **groups** in a table. Each group contained elements with similar chemical properties. This made it much easier for chemists to work out what to expect when they reacted elements with each other. The modern **periodic table**, on the next page, is based on the observations of Mendeleev.

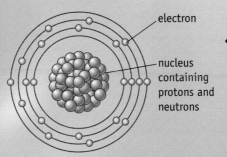

electron

nucleus containing protons and neutrons

*This is a model of a scandium atom. This particular atom has 21 protons and 24 neutrons. Its 21 electrons are arranged in four energy levels, or shells, around the nucleus.*

# CHAPTER 2

# The periodic table and the transition metals

Chemists built on Mendeleev's work and eventually produced the modern **periodic table**, which you can see here. Each row in the table is called a **period**, and the elements in a period are arranged in order of increasing **atomic number** (the atomic number is the number of **protons** in the **nucleus**). Each column in the table is called a **group**. Within each group, the **elements** have similar chemical properties to each other. For example, all the elements in group 1 are very reactive, soft metals, and all the elements in group 0 are very unreactive gases. It is called the periodic table because these different chemical properties occur, regularly or periodically.

▼ This is the periodic table of the elements. The transition metals consist of ten groups of elements, which lie between groups 2 and 3.

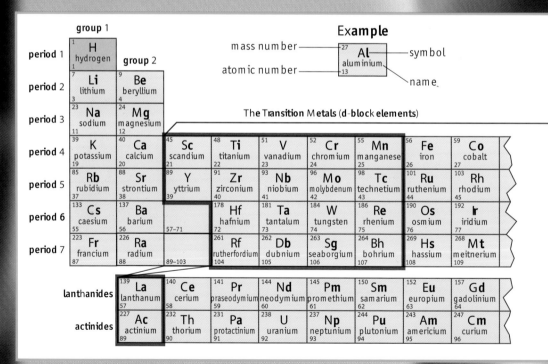

# The transition metals

The transition metals are the big block of elements in the middle of the periodic table, between group 2 (the alkaline earth metals) and group 3. They have many properties in common, such as high melting and boiling points, but they are not identical to each other. Tungsten, for example, has the highest melting point of any metal, yet mercury is the only metal that is liquid at room temperature. The transition metals tend to have high **densities** and they often produce coloured **compounds**. Unlike the other elements in the periodic table, the transition metals in each group may be less like each other, and more like the elements either side of them. However, they do have some things in common, usually the formulae of the compounds they form with other elements.

In this book, you are going to find out about titanium, tungsten and the other transition metals in the first five groups, the compounds they make, and many of their uses.

## Key

- metals
- metalloids
- non-metals

| | | group 3 | group 4 | group 5 | group 6 | group 7 | group 0 |
|---|---|---|---|---|---|---|---|
| | | | | | | | 4 **He** helium 2 |
| | | 11 **B** boron 5 | 12 **C** carbon 6 | 14 **N** nitrogen 7 | 16 **O** oxygen 8 | 19 **F** fluorine 9 | 20 **Ne** neon 10 |
| | | 27 **Al** aluminium 13 | 28 **Si** silicon 14 | 31 **P** phosphorus 15 | 32 **S** sulphur 16 | 35 **Cl** chlorine 17 | 40 **Ar** argon 18 |
| 59 **Ni** nickel 28 | 64 **Cu** copper 29 | 65 **Zn** zinc 30 | 70 **Ga** gallium 31 | 73 **Ge** germanium 32 | 75 **As** arsenic 33 | 79 **Se** selenium 34 | 80 **Br** bromine 35 | 84 **Kr** krypton 36 |
| 106 **Pd** palladium 46 | 108 **Ag** silver 47 | 112 **Cd** cadmium 48 | 115 **In** indium 49 | 119 **Sn** tin 50 | 122 **Sb** antimony 51 | 128 **Te** tellurium 52 | 127 **I** iodine 53 | 131 **Xe** xenon 54 |
| 195 **Pt** platinum 78 | 197 **Au** gold 79 | 201 **Hg** mercury 80 | 204 **Tl** thallium 81 | 207 **Pb** lead 82 | 209 **Bi** bismuth 83 | 209 **Po** polonium 84 | 210 **At** astatine 85 | 222 **Rn** radon 86 |
| 281 **Ds** darmstadtium 110 | 280 **Rg** roentgenium 111 | 285 **Uub** ununbium 112 | | 289 **Uuq** ununquadium 114 | | 292 **Uuh** ununhexium 116 | | |

f block

| 159 **Tb** terbium 65 | 163 **Dy** dysprosium 66 | 165 **Ho** holmium 67 | 167 **Er** erbium 68 | 169 **Tm** thulium 69 | 173 **Yb** ytterbium 70 | 175 **Lu** lutetium 71 |
|---|---|---|---|---|---|---|
| 247 **Bk** berkelium 97 | 251 **Cf** californium 98 | 252 **Es** einsteinium 99 | 257 **Fm** fermium 100 | 258 **Md** mendelevium 101 | 259 **No** nobelium 102 | 262 **Lr** lawrencium 103 |

# General features of the transition metals

The transition metals are malleable, which means that they are easily bent or hammered into shape, and they are good conductors of electricity and heat. They tend to be hard, strong and tough, and they have other properties that are extremely useful to us. The transition metals are similar to each other because one of their **electron** shells, called the d sub-shell, is not completely filled with electrons.

**Groups** 1 and 2 contain most of the other familiar metals, so it is helpful to see how the transition metals compare with them. Group 1 includes lithium, sodium and potassium, and group 2 includes magnesium and calcium.

## High melting and boiling points

If we ignore beryllium in group 2, which has unusually high melting and boiling points, nearly all the transition metals have higher melting and boiling points than the metals in groups 1 and 2.

*The boiling points of nearly all the transition metals are much higher than the boiling points of the metals in group 2. The melting points of the metals in group 1 are even lower.* ▶

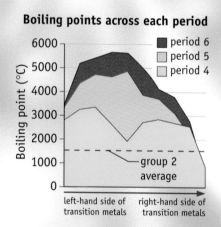

**Boiling points across each period**

## Low reactivity

The transition metals are much less reactive than the metals in groups 1 and 2. Whereas potassium bursts into flames in water and caesium explodes violently in it, the transition metals react only slowly with water, if at all. Few of the transition metals react quickly with air and acids.

## High densities

The elements in groups 1 and 2 have low **densities**. Lithium, sodium and potassium will even float on water, but the transition metals generally have high densities. Osmium and iridium have the highest densities of any element, and a litre of osmium or iridium has a mass of 22.5 kg, which is similar to the mass of a golden retriever dog!

*The densities of all the transition metals are much higher than the densities of the metals in group 2. The densities of the metals in group 1 are even lower.* ▶

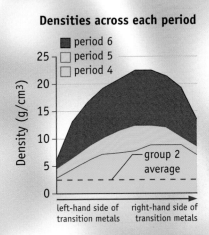

**Densities across each period**

## Catalysts and colours

Metals lose electrons from their outer shells when they react with non-metals, such as oxygen. When they do this, they form electrically charged particles called **ions**. Metal ions are positively charged. Group 1 metals always form ions with a single positive charge, like the $Na^+$ ions formed by sodium. Group 2 metals always form ions with two positive charges, such as magnesium ions, $Mg^{2+}$. However, transition metals can form more than one type of ion. As a result, transition metals and their **compounds** frequently make good **catalysts**, which means that they can speed up **reactions** without being used up.

Transition metals can also form different compounds with the same non-metal. For example, vanadium and oxygen react together to make vanadium oxide. However, as there are several forms of it, chemists use roman numbers to tell them apart. So, $V_2O_3$ is vanadium(III) oxide (pronounced 'vanadium three oxide') and it contains $V^{3+}$ ions. However, $V_2O_5$ is vanadium(V) oxide (pronounced 'vanadium five oxide') and it contain $V^{5+}$ ions. Transition metal compounds are usually coloured because of the way light is absorbed by the ions in them. Vanadium(III) oxide is black, but vanadium(V) oxide is orange.

# Isotopes and radioactivity

## Isotopes

**Atoms** of an **element** always have the same number of **protons** in their **nucleus**. Scandium atoms, for example, always have 21 protons. However, scandium atoms do not always have the same number of **neutrons** in their nucleus.

▲ *This is the warning symbol for radioactive materials.*

**Isotopes** of an element have atoms that have the same number of protons and **electrons**, but different numbers of neutrons. The most abundant, or common, isotope of scandium is scandium-45. The nucleus of a scandium-45 atom has 21 protons as you would expect, and it has 24 neutrons. However, there are several other isotopes of scandium, including scandium-44, which only has 23 neutrons. But, because scandium-44 still has 21 protons and 21 electrons, it behaves chemically just like scandium-45.

## Chemical symbols

The full chemical symbol for scandium-45 is $^{45}_{21}$Sc. In a chemical symbol like this, the bottom number is called the **proton number** or **atomic number**. It shows how many protons there are in the nucleus. The top number is called the **mass number**, and it shows the sum of the number of protons and the number of neutrons. To work out how many neutrons there are in the nucleus, just subtract the bottom number from the top number!

## Half-life

It is possible for the nucleus of atom to break up or **decay** into smaller pieces. Nobody can say when an individual atom will decay, but by studying huge numbers of atoms it is possible to say how long it takes for half of them to decay. The time it takes for half the atoms in an isotope to decay is called the **half-life** of the isotope. This time cannot be changed by any chemical **reactions** or by heating or cooling.

Some isotopes have a very unstable nucleus. They decay very quickly and have very short half-lives. The half-life of scandium-44, for example, is a little less than four hours, but other isotopes may have half-lives of only a fraction of a second. Scandium-45 and other naturally occurring isotopes are much more stable and may have half-lives of millions of years.

## Radiation

When an unstable nucleus breaks up, it decays to become an isotope of another element or another isotope of the same element. **Radiation** is given out in this process. There are different types of radiation, including particles shot out of the nucleus at high speed, and a high-energy form of light called gamma radiation. Depending on the type of radiation produced, it can pass through the air, plastic and metal, and into our bodies. Radiation can cause cancer if it damages the DNA in our cells, so laws protect us from over-exposure to **radioactive** chemicals. However, radiation can be useful to us if it is carefully controlled. For example, technetium-99, an isotope of a transition metal discussed in this book, is used in some types of medical scans. Also, scandium-46 is used by the oil industry as a **tracer**.

▼ *Different types of radiation can go through different materials. Alpha (α) radiation (helium nuclei) is stopped by paper. Beta (β) radiation (electrons) travels through paper and sheets of aluminium. Gamma (γ) radiation (a type of high-energy light) travels through paper, aluminium and thin sheets of lead. It may need several metres of concrete or very thick lead to stop it.*

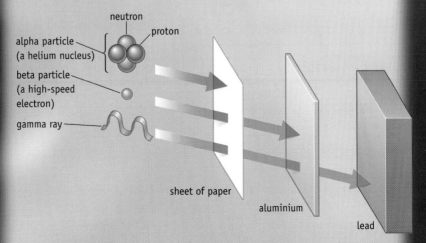

neutron

proton

alpha particle
(a helium nucleus)

beta particle
(a high-speed electron)

gamma ray

sheet of paper

aluminium

lead

# Artificial transition metal elements

Uranium **atoms** are the heaviest natural atoms, with 92 **protons** in their **nuclei**. Atoms with more protons, called transuranic **elements**, have to be made artificially (in a laboratory) by converting one element into another. The ancient alchemists tried to turn lead into gold without any success. This was because it is not possible to convert one element into another by chemical **reactions** – you can only turn one element into another by a nuclear reaction, such as a nuclear bomb.

When a radioactive atom **decays**, its nucleus splits apart to make a new nucleus and it gives out **radiation**. A new element made this way has a smaller number of particles in its nucleus than the original element. For example, uranium-238 is the most abundant **isotope** of the transition metal uranium, and it gradually decays to produce another element called thorium-234. Each time a uranium-238 nucleus breaks apart, it produces **alpha radiation**. This is caused by a small particle called an alpha particle, which is fired from the nucleus at high speed. Alpha particles are like helium atoms with their electrons removed.

▲ *This is the huge mushroom-shaped cloud from the world's first hydrogen bomb, detonated at Eniwetok atoll in the Pacific Ocean on 1 November, 1952. Nuclear reactions during the explosion produced two new elements – einsteinium and fermium.*

*The word equation for the decay of uranium-238 is:*

uranium-238 → thorium-234 + helium-4 (an alpha particle)

*In this nuclear reaction, one large nucleus splits into two smaller ones.*

To get a new artificial element with a bigger nucleus, you need to do this process in reverse. Scientists strip the **electrons** from atoms to produce electrically charged particles called **ions**. They get these ions moving at tremendously high speeds in a machine called a particle accelerator, and then fire them into a metal target. If the scientists are lucky, an ion and a target atom stick together to make a new atom with a much larger nucleus. For example, the transition metal bohrium was first made by smashing chromium ions into bismuth atoms.

*The word equation for making bohrium from chromium and bismuth is:*

chromium-54 + bismuth-209 → bohrium-262 + neutron $(_0^1 n)$

*A neutron is also produced in this nuclear reaction.*
*The large bohrium atom is very unstable and decays very quickly – the **half-life** of bohrium-262 is just 0.1 seconds.*

Nine artificial transition metals have been made this way but the amounts are tiny, often just one or a few atoms at a time (see pages 14–15). In addition, the atoms are very unstable with extremely short half-lives, so very little is known about their chemistry. However, chemists are confident that they will have similar properties to the other transition metals in the **periodic table**.

| 261 **Rf** rutherfordium 104 | **rutherfordium** symbol: Rf • atomic number: 104 • period 7 |

Rutherfordium was first made in 1964 when Russian scientists smashed neon **ions** into plutonium. They called it kurchatovium, after the Head of Soviet Nuclear Research, Igor Kurchatov. Five years later, American scientists produced four different **isotopes** of the new **element** by firing carbon ions at californium targets. They called it rutherfordium after Lord Rutherford, who was given the Nobel Prize for Chemistry in 1908 for his work on **radioactivity**. The element was also called unnilquadium (pronounced 'yoo-nil-kwad-ee-um'), which means 'one-zero-four', until the International Union of Pure and Applied Chemistry (IUPAC) adopted the name rutherfordium in 1997.

*This is Sigurd Hofmann of the Institute for Heavy Ion Research (GSI) at Darmstadt in Germany. Six new elements were discovered here between 1981 and 1996.* ▶

| 262 **Db** dubnium 105 | **dubnium** symbol: Db • atomic number: 105 • period 7 |

Dubnium was first made in 1967 when Russian scientists bombarded americium with neon ions. They called it dubnium after Dubna, the city in which the research was carried out. American scientists also made it three years later by smashing nitrogen ions into californium. They wanted to call it hahnium after Otto Hahn, a German scientist. The element was temporarily called unnilpentium (pronounced 'yoo-nil-pent-ee-um'), which means 'one-zero-five', until IUPAC approved the name dubnium in 1997.

| 263 Sg seaborgium 106 | **seaborgium** |
|---|---|
| | *symbol: Sg • atomic number: 106 • period 7* |

Seaborgium was first made in 1974 when American scientists fired oxygen ions into californium. They called it seaborgium after Glenn Seaborg, an American nuclear physicist and Nobel Prize winner. Seaborg was involved in discovering several transuranic elements, so the name seemed a good choice. However, IUPAC was not keen on the name seaborgium because Seaborg was alive at the time, and for a while the element was called unnilhexium (pronounced 'yoo-nil-hex-ee-um'), which means 'one-zero-six'. IUPAC eventually allowed the name seaborgium just two years before Seaborg's death in 1999.

| 264 Bh bohrium 107 | **bohrium** |
|---|---|
| | *symbol: Bh • atomic number: 107 • period 7* |

Scientists at the Institute for Heavy Ion Research in Germany first made bohrium in 1981, when they bombarded bismuth with chromium ions. They wanted to call it nielsbohrium, after Niels Bohr, the Danish physicist who developed important theories about the structure of the atom and who won the Nobel Prize for Physics in 1922. IUPAC was not happy to include Bohr's first name in the name of the new element, and it was temporarily called unnilseptium (pronounced 'yoo-nil-sept-ee-um'), which means 'one-zero-seven'. The name bohrium was agreed in 1997.

*Glenn Seaborg discovered plutonium in 1940. He received the Nobel Prize for Chemistry, when he was just 39, for his research into transuranic elements. Seaborgium is named in his honour.* ▶

# First group: scandium

| 45 Sc scandium 21 | scandium<br>symbol: Sc • atomic number: 21 • period 4 |
|---|---|

Scandium is a silvery metal. It reacts with oxygen in the air, gradually turning a light yellow colour, and it burns when heated to form scandium oxide. Unlike most of the transition metals, scandium reacts with water when it is warmed, and produces scandium hydroxide and hydrogen. It also reacts with acids to produce scandium salts and hydrogen.

**Who discovered it?**   Lars Nilson, a Swedish chemist, discovered scandium in 1879. He studied two **minerals**, gadolinite and euxenite. Johan Gadolin had discovered yttrium (just below scandium in the **periodic table**) in gadolinite just over a hundred years earlier, but Nilson also managed to **extract** the oxide of another previously unknown metal. Nilson was unable to isolate the pure metal, which he called scandium after Scandinavia, but he learned a lot about its **compounds**. Scandium metal was first isolated in 1937 by passing electricity through a mixture of molten scandium chloride, lithium chloride and potassium chloride.

**Where is it found?**   Scandium is not found naturally as the free metal. It is quite rare and makes up barely 0.0005 per cent of the Earth's crust, but it is found in small amounts in many minerals such as gadolinite. Thortveitite contains up to 40 per cent scandium oxide, but it is a rare mineral and most scandium is extracted from the waste left over from uranium **refining**. This is not a problem, however, because scandium has few applications and only a few kilograms are needed each year. Scandium metal is produced by reacting scandium fluoride with a reactive metal, such as calcium.

**What are its main uses?**   Scandium is added to other metals to form very strong and light **alloys**.

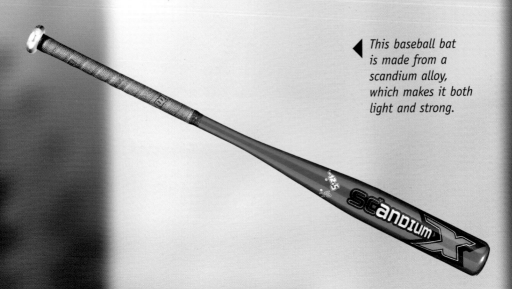

*This baseball bat is made from a scandium alloy, which makes it both light and strong.*

## Bicycles, bats and oil

Scandium-aluminium alloys are used to make very strong, and very expensive, sports equipment. These include bicycle frames and baseball bats. As little as 2 per cent scandium in the alloy significantly increases its strength, which allows the weight of the frame or bat to be reduced, but it costs several times more than ordinary alloys. Some firearms manufacturers also use scandium alloys because they are as strong as steel or titanium but much lighter.

The oil industry uses **radioactive** scandium-46, $^{46}_{21}$Sc, as a **tracer** to check the flow of oil in oil fields. The tracer is added to the oil underground, and then the **radiation** is measured at different times and places in the oil field. Engineers can use the information to tell how and where the oil is flowing without having to drill lots of new holes into the ground.

Mercury vapour lamps produce a bluish light, but when scandium iodide is added to them they produce a bright white light that is similar to daylight. Television lighting engineers use these 'metal halide' lamps to light TV studios or to boost the natural light outside, especially at night. As the balance of colours in the light is similar to daylight, the colours in the television picture appear correctly.

# First group: yttrium

| 89 | Y | **yttrium** |
|---|---|---|
| 39 | yttrium | symbol: Y • atomic number: 39 • period 5 |

Yttrium (pronounced 'ittree-um') is a soft, silvery metal. Its surface is protected by a layer of yttrium oxide which prevents it reacting with air and water at room temperature. However, when it is heated it will react with water, it will burn in air to form yttrium(III) oxide, and it will react with acids.

**Who discovered it?**   The Finnish chemist, Johan Gadolin, discovered yttrium in 1794 – the same year in which the great French chemist Antoine Lavoisier was executed by the guillotine. Gadolin studied a mineral, originally called ytterbite but now called gadolinite, found in a quarry near Ytterby in Sweden. He was able to isolate the oxide of a previously unknown metal, which he called yttrium, after Ytterby where it was found. Friedrich Wöhler first isolated yttrium in 1828 by heating yttrium(III) chloride with potassium.

*The word equation for Wöhler's method of isolating yttrium is:*

yttrium(III) + potassium → yttrium + potassium
chloride                           chloride

*This works because potassium is more reactive than yttrium.*

**Where is it found?**   Yttrium is not found naturally as the free metal. It makes up about 0.004 per cent of the Earth's crust and it is found in small amounts in many **minerals**. Monazite and xenotime are important sources of yttrium, but bastnasite is its main **ore**, and comes mainly from China and the USA. These ores usually contain other metals, called rare earth metals. It is quite difficult to separate the yttrium from the other metals, and only a few tonnes of yttrium are produced each year.

*What are its main uses?*   Yttrium is mixed with other metals, particularly aluminium, chromium and magnesium, to produce various **alloys**. These are often strong, and resist wear and **corrosion** even at high temperatures. They are used as coatings in gas turbines, which get very hot, and in long-life spark plugs for car engines.

## Let there be light

**Phosphors** are chemicals that give off light when they are exposed to **radiation** such as electron beams. They are used to produce the images on television screens and computer monitors. The red phosphor contains yttrium vanadate or yttrium(III) oxide, and a rare earth metal called europium.

Yttrium aluminium garnet (YAG) is a **compound** of yttrium, aluminium and oxygen. YAG forms crystals that are widely used in **lasers**. These lasers are often used in outdoor laser shows because their green light can be seen for up to 50 km. Lasers containing YAG crystals with a little neodymium in them are widely used in industry to mark, cut and join metals.

▼ Lasers using crystals containing yttrium produce a bright green light. They are used for special effects in outdoor laser shows, such as at this concert near the Egyptian pyramids at Giza.

# First group: lanthanum and actinium

Most of the transition metals belong to a part of the **periodic table** called the 'd-block'. This is because (apart from zinc, cadmium and mercury in the tenth group) one of their shells, called the d sub-shell, is only partly filled with **electrons**. When you look at some periodic tables, you will find two further **elements** immediately below scandium and yttrium. These are lanthanum and actinium. They actually belong to another block in the periodic table, called the 'f-block'. The elements in the f-block are sometimes called the inner transition metals. There are two **periods** or rows of elements in the f-block. The elements in the same period as lanthanum are called the lanthanides, and those in the same period as actinium are called the actinides.

You can find a little information about lanthanum and actinium here, but there is more information about them in another book in this series, *Uranium and the Rare Earth Metals*.

▼ *Photographers use lights that contain lanthanum bulbs in their studios.*

| 139 **La** lanthanum 57 | **lanthanum** |
|---|---|
| | symbol: La • atomic number: 57 • period 6 |

Lanthanum is a soft, silvery metal. It is so soft that it can be cut with a knife. Unlike the other elements in this book, it is quite reactive. Lanthanum reacts with oxygen in the air, and when heated it will burn in air to produce lanthanum(III) oxide. It also reacts with water and dilute acids.

*Where is it found?*   Lanthanum is not found naturally as the free metal, but various **minerals** contain it. These include a type of sand called monazite and a mineral called bastnasite, which is also the main **ore** of yttrium.

*What are its main uses?*   Lanthanum is a component of **alloys** such as misch metal, which is used in the flints for cigarette lighters. Lanthanum **compounds** are used in studio lights and some types of glass.

| 227 **Ac** actinium 89 | **actinium** |
|---|---|
| | symbol: Ac • atomic number: 89 • period 7 |

Actinium is a rare, silvery metal. Like lanthanum it is quite soft, but unlike lanthanum it glows in the dark! This is because it is intensely **radioactive**. Actinium reacts slowly with the oxygen in the air, it burns to produce actinium(III) oxide when heated, and it reacts with water.

*Where is it found?*   Actinium is found naturally in uranium ores, such as pitchblende. However, only tiny amounts can be recovered from this. It takes 10 tonnes of uranium ore to produce just one gram of actinium. Actinium can be **extracted** from nuclear waste, and it can be made artificially by smashing high-speed **neutrons** into radium.

*What are its main uses?*   It is mainly used in scientific research because it is such a powerful emitter of **radiation**.

# CHAPTER 4

# Second group: titanium

| 48 **Ti** titanium 22 | **titanium** *symbol: Ti • atomic number: 22 • period 4* |
|---|---|

Titanium is a strong, silvery-white metal with a low **density**. A very thin layer of titanium(IV) oxide forms on the surface of titanium, and this stops the metal underneath reacting with air or water unless it is heated. If it is heated in air, titanium burns vigorously with a white flame, producing titanium(IV) oxide and titanium(III) nitride. Titanium reacts with steam to produce titanium(IV) oxide and hydrogen, and it will react with dilute acids if they are hot.

**Who discovered it?** Titanium was discovered in 1791 by an English vicar, William Gregor. He examined a black mineral, now called ilmenite, which he found in the local river. Gregor found that it contained an unusual red-brown metal oxide that dissolved in sulphuric acid to produce a yellow solution, which then turned purple when iron was added. Martin Klaproth, a German chemist, rediscovered the **element** four years later in a **mineral** called rutile. He called it titanium after the Titans, the first gods in Greek mythology. Klaproth tried unsuccessfully to isolate the new element, but a Swedish chemist called Jöns Berzelius managed to isolate impure titanium in 1825. Matthew Hunter, a New Zealander working in the USA, first isolated pure titanium in 1910 by reacting titanium chloride with sodium.

**Where is it found?** Titanium is the ninth most abundant element and makes up 0.44 per cent of the Earth's crust. It is not found in its native state as the free metal, but it is found almost everywhere in various minerals. Ilmenite and rutile, which both contain titanium(IV) oxide, are the main **ores** of titanium. Ilmenite provides about 90 per cent of the world's titanium, and over four million tonnes of titanium ores are mined each year, mainly in Australia, Canada and South Africa.

**What are its main uses?** Most titanium ore is processed to make titanium **compounds** for pigments and paints, and only about 55,000 tonnes of the metal itself are produced each year.

## Extraction of titanium

Titanium is **extracted** using the Kroll Process, invented by William Kroll in 1932. Titanium(IV) chloride is heated to over 1000°C with a reactive metal such as magnesium to produce titanium metal. An unreactive atmosphere of argon gas is needed to protect the metal from gases in the air. Scientists working at the University of Cambridge have patented a new, much simpler way to produce titanium, called the Fray–Farthing–Chen (FFC) Process. In this process, titanium(IV) oxide is mixed with molten calcium chloride, and electricity is passed through the mixture. This removes oxygen from the titanium(IV) oxide, leaving titanium metal behind. The FFC Process will allow titanium to be produced much more cheaply in the future.

*The word equation for producing titanium using the Kroll process is:*

titanium(IV) chloride + magnesium → titanium + magnesium chloride

▼ *The Guggenheim Museum in Bilbao, Spain, has a steel frame covered with 33,000 titanium panels just 3 mm thick.*

# Uses of titanium

The **density** of titanium is 45 per cent less than the density of steel, but it is just as strong as steel. This means that it is a light but strong metal. Unlike steel, titanium does not rust. This makes it a metal with some very useful properties. Its only real drawback is that it is much more expensive than steel, but this may change. The development of new ways to produce it may bring the cost down and titanium could be the material of the future!

## Strong but light

Titanium and titanium **alloys** are used in the aircraft industry where it is important to keep the weight of materials down without losing any of the strength. Titanium alloys also keep their strength at high temperatures, so they are used in racing car engines and missiles. Titanium containing 6 per cent aluminium and 4 per cent vanadium is up to eight times stronger than pure titanium. This alloy is widely used to make various aircraft parts such as the wings, fuselage (main body) and landing gear.

Titanium may be used on its own when resistance to **corrosion** is more important than strength. Artificial hip joints are made from pure titanium, as the metal will not react with body tissues and liquids.

## Whiter than white

Titanium(IV) oxide, $TiO^2$, forms about 95 per cent of the titanium used in the world. It is also called titanium white because it is a brilliant white solid, and it has some surprising uses. Titanium(IV) oxide is the **pigment** in white paints. It is used to whiten textiles, paper and plastics. As titanium(IV) oxide is not poisonous, it has many other uses too. It is used in cosmetics, including make-up such as eye shadow and lipstick. It is also widely used to colour toothpaste, tablets and pills. Sun blocks often contain titanium(IV) oxide mixed with zinc oxide. Food manufacturers use it where a bright white colour is needed in sweets and other foods, such as coffee whitener.

◀ *The SR-71 Blackbird aircraft flew at 3200 km/h, more than three times the speed of sound, at altitudes of 26 km. They were built almost entirely of titanium and titanium alloys.*

## Sky writing

Titanium(IV) chloride, $TiCl_4$, is one of the substances produced during the extraction of titanium from its **ores** using a method called the Kroll Process. It is a smelly, colourless liquid that needs to be handled with care. This is because it reacts with water vapour in the air to produce acidic fumes of hydrogen chloride. The **reaction** also produces tiny particles of titanium(IV) oxide that form white clouds. This may seem pointless, but sky-writers use titanium(IV) chloride to write messages in the air. They spray it from canisters attached to the aircraft, and it leaves a white trail of titanium(IV) oxide. Titanium(IV) chloride is also used in smoke bombs and for special effects in films.

*The word equation for the reaction of titanium(IV) chloride with water is:*

titanium(IV) + water → titanium(IV) + hydrogen
chloride           oxide      chloride

# Second group: zirconium

| 91 | Zr | **zirconium** |
|---|---|---|
| 40 | zirconium | *symbol: Zr • atomic number: 40 • period 5* |

Zirconium is a shiny grey-white metal. Very pure zirconium is soft, but impure zirconium is hard, **brittle** and difficult to work. The surface of the metal is protected by a thin layer of zirconium(IV) oxide. This stops the metal from reacting with air, water or dilute acids. However, zirconium will burn in air when heated strongly, to produce zirconium(IV) oxide.

*Who discovered it?*   Zirconium was discovered in 1789 by the German chemist, Martin Klaproth. He studied some crystals of a precious stone called zircon, and **extracted** a previously unknown metal oxide. Klaproth called this new metal zirconium after the **mineral** he found it in (the word zircon comes from an Arabic word meaning golden coloured). The Swedish chemist Jöns Berzelius isolated zirconium 35 years later when he heated potassium zirconium fluoride with potassium metal.

*Where is it found?*   Zirconium is not found naturally as the free metal, and it makes up just 0.015 per cent of the Earth's crust. The main zirconium **ores** are zircon (zirconium silicate, $ZrSiO_4$) and baddelyite (zirconium(IV) oxide, $ZrO_2$). About one million tonnes of these minerals are mined in the world each year, mainly in South Africa, Australia and the USA, and about 7000 tonnes of zirconium is produced from them.

Zirconium and hafnium are nearly always found together. They are very similar chemically, and even their **atoms** are almost identical in size. This makes it is very difficult to separate the two metals from each other. As a result, zirconium often contains up to 1 per cent hafnium, and hafnium often contains up to 2 per cent zirconium.

Zirconium is extracted from its ores in several complex steps. The final stage in extraction uses the Kroll Process, invented by William Kroll in 1932 to produce titanium metal, and modified by him in 1945 to produce zirconium.

**What are its main uses?**  About 90 per cent of the zirconium produced is used by the nuclear industry.

## Useful and beautiful

The nuclear **reaction** in nuclear power stations needs high-speed **neutrons**. These neutrons are released from uranium atoms that are contained in the fuel rods of a nuclear power station. This uranium is combined with zirconium to form the fuel rods. Zirconium is an ideal material for this as high-speed neutrons pass very easily through the metal.

As zirconium resists **corrosion** very well, it is used in **alloys** to make surgical instruments and equipment for the chemical industry.

Simulated diamonds for jewellery are made from crystals of 'cubic zirconia', a **compound** of zirconium(IV) oxide and yttrium(III) oxide. They are not artificial diamonds (these are made from pure carbon) but they look very similar to the real thing, and they are a lot cheaper!

◄ *This is a used nuclear fuel rod in a water-filled cooling pond. Its blue glow comes from radiation passing through the water. Fuel rods are made from an alloy of zirconium and hafnium, which easily lets through high-speed neutrons from the fuel.*

# Second group: hafnium

| 178 | | hafnium |
|---|---|---|
| **Hf** | | *symbol: Hf • atomic number: 72 • period 6* |
| hafnium | | |
| 72 | | |

Hafnium is a strong, silvery metal. A thin layer of hafnium (IV) oxide forms on the surface, and this stops the metal reacting with air, water or acids. However, hafnium will burn in air to make hafnium(IV) oxide if heated strongly enough.

## Looking for a missing element

Chemists knew there should be another **element** below zirconium in the **periodic table**. Dirk Coster and Georg von Hevesy, who worked in Neils Bohr's laboratory in Copenhagen, were asked to look for the missing element in **minerals** containing zirconium. They used a method called X-ray spectroscopy to study zircon, a mineral that contains zirconium silicate, and discovered hafnium in 1923. Hafnium was later isolated in 1925 by Anton van Arkel and Jan deBoer, who passed hafnium(IV) chloride vapour over hot tungsten metal. The name hafnium comes from 'Hafnia', which is the Latin name for Copenhagen.

*Where is it found?* Hafnium is not found naturally as the free metal, and it makes up just 0.0003 per cent of the Earth's crust. Hafnium and zirconium are nearly always found together because they are very similar. The main zirconium **ore**, zircon, contains about 2 per cent hafnium. Alvite is a mineral consisting of zircon with up to 10 per cent of the zirconium **atoms** swapped for hafnium atoms. About 1 million tonnes of these minerals are mined in the world each year, mainly in South Africa, Australia and the USA. Around 50 tonnes of hafnium are produced each year.

*Hafnium is a strong silvery metal. It is often mixed with other metals such as iron and titanium to make alloys, and it is used in the control rods for nuclear power stations.*

Some heat-protecting systems of spacecraft contain hafnium carbide, as this can resist the temperatures of 2700° C that are reached on re-entry into the Earth's atmosphere.

It is very difficult to separate hafnium and zirconium from each other. Hafnium is separated from zirconium during the extraction of zirconium from its ores. In the final stage, hafnium metal is produced by heating hafnium(IV) chloride with a very reactive metal, such as sodium or magnesium.

**What are its main uses?** Hafnium is used to make the control rods for nuclear power stations. Although the nuclear **reaction** needs high-speed **neutrons** to keep going, the rate of the reaction needs to be controlled by stopping some of the neutrons. Hafnium is very good at doing this, and it is also very strong and does not corrode in the reactor.

Hafnium carbide, HfC, melts at 3890 °C. This is the highest melting point of any compound consisting of just two elements. It means that hafnium carbide can be used in materials that resist very high temperatures, called refractory materials. These are used in rocket motors and the heat shields for spacecraft.

# CHAPTER 5

# Third group: vanadium

| 51 | V | vanadium |
|----|---|----------|
| | vanadium | *symbol: V • atomic number: 23 • period 4* |
| 23 | | |

Vanadium is a soft, silvery-white metal. It does not react with water or acids, but it will react with oxygen in the air to produce vanadium(V) oxide if heated strongly.

**Who discovered it?**   Vanadium was first discovered 1801 by Andrés Manuel del Río, a Mexican professor of mineralogy. He isolated a red solid from a brown **mineral** that is now called vanadinite. At first he thought he had discovered a new metal, which he called erythronium. Unfortunately, del Río got cold feet about his discovery and decided that it was really only lead chromate. A Swedish chemist called Nils Sefström rediscovered vanadium nearly 30 years later in 1830. He named it after Vanadis, the Norse goddess of beauty. A year later, the German chemist Friedrich Wöhler showed that del Río's erythronium was vanadium after all. An English chemist, Sir Henry Roscoe, first isolated vanadium in 1867 when he reacted vanadium chloride with hydrogen.

**Where is it found?**   Vanadium is not found naturally as the free metal, and it makes up about 0.02 per cent of the Earth's crust. It is found in bauxite (aluminium **ore**) and crude oil, but its main ores are carnotite, vanadinite and patronite. Ores containing about 40,000 tonnes of vanadium are mined each year, mainly in China, Russia and South Africa.

Vanadium is **extracted** in different ways depending upon which ore is used. Each involves several steps. However, they eventually produce vanadium **compounds** that form vanadium(V) oxide when heated strongly. Some of this vanadium(V) oxide is used to make vanadium metal by heating it with reactive metals such as calcium and aluminium.

**What are its main uses?**   Vanadium is used to make **alloys** that are used in the steel industry, the aircraft industry and the chemical industry.

## Ferrovanadium

Over 80 per cent of the vanadium(V) oxide produced is used to make ferrovanadium. This is an alloy of iron and vanadium that is widely used in steel making. Ferrovanadium is made by adding vanadium(V) oxide to a mixture of molten iron, aluminium and calcium oxide. These react together to produce vanadium metal, and this mixes with the iron to form the ferrovanadium.

## Engine parts

Chrome vanadium steel, which contains up to 10 per cent chromium and 5 per cent vanadium, is strong, tough and resistant to rusting. It is used in axles and engine parts for cars, and tools. Kitchen knives made from it are very tough and keep their sharp edge. The aircraft industry uses titanium alloys containing up to 15 per cent vanadium because they are very strong for their weight and are ideal for making wings and engine parts.

## An important catalyst

Vanadium(V) oxide is the **catalyst** used in the contact process for making sulphuric acid. One of the stages involves reacting sulphur dioxide with oxygen to make sulphur trioxide, and vanadium(V) oxide speeds up this **reaction** without being used up. Another vanadium catalyst is important in the production of adipic acid, also known as hexanedioic acid, which is used in the manufacture of nylon.

◀ *This tool is made from chrome vanadium steel and is strong, tough and resistant to rusting.*

# Third group: niobium

| 93 | **Nb** | **niobium** |
|----|--------|-------------|
| | niobium | symbol: Nb • atomic number: 41 • period 5 |
| 41 | | |

Niobium is a soft, silvery metal. When its surface is cut, the metal beneath slowly reacts with oxygen in the air to produce a thin layer of niobium oxide that gives it a bluish tinge. This protective layer stops the metal from reacting any further. Niobium does not react with air, water or dilute acids.

*Who discovered it?*    Niobium was discovered in 1801 by the English chemist, Charles Hatchett. He isolated a new metal oxide from a black **mineral** called columbite, but he could not isolate the free metal. However, Hatchett was confident that he had discovered a new **element**, which he called columbium. A year later, a Swedish chemist called Anders Ekeberg discovered another new element in a similar mineral. He called the new element tantalum, after King Tantalus in Greek mythology. Unfortunately, an important English chemist, Charles Wollaston, studied columbite in 1809 and mistakenly announced that columbium and tantalum were the same metal.

Heinrich Rose, a German chemist, re-examined Ekeberg's mineral in 1844. He realized that it contained not only tantalum but another new metal. Rose called this new metal niobium, after Niobe, the daughter of Tantalus. Rose's niobium and Hatchett's columbium turned out to be the same element, but both names were common until the name niobium was agreed in 1950. Impure niobium was isolated in 1866, and the pure metal was isolated 40 years later by a German chemist called Werner von Bolton.

*Where is it found?*    Niobium is not found naturally as the free metal, and it makes up just 0.002 per cent of the Earth's crust. The most important **ores** of niobium are columbite (niobite) and pyrochlore, and ores containing over 30,000 tonnes of niobium are mined each year, mostly in Brazil. The ores are processed to concentrate the niobium **compounds** in them, but less than 10 per cent is processed further to make pure niobium. Most of the processed ore is used to make a mixture of iron and niobium called ferroniobium, which is used in steel making. The rest is converted to niobium oxide, which is then heated with sodium to produce niobium.

*What are its main uses?*  Niobium is used for many things but especially in making very strong steel.

## Beautiful and useful

As niobium is an unreactive metal, it is often used for earrings because it does not react with skin and other body tissues. Its bluish tinge makes the jewellery look attractive, too. Niobium is mixed with iron and other metals to make the stainless steel for some car exhaust systems. It is also a component of some of the **corrosion**-resistant **alloys** for nuclear reactors, and heat-resistant 'superalloys' used in aircraft engines and rockets. However, its biggest single use is to make strong steels. These contain up to 1 per cent niobium, and are used in all sorts of things including cars, ships, oilrigs and gas pipelines.

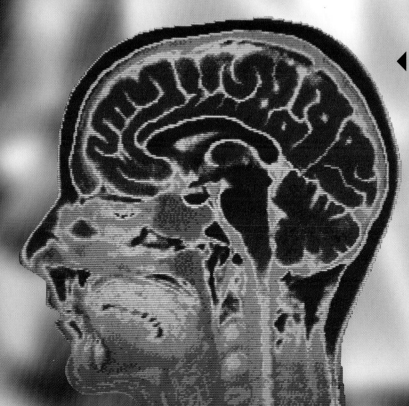

*The magnetic resonance imaging scanners used in hospitals contain superconducting magnets made from niobium-titanium alloy. MRI scanners produce very detailed pictures of the insides of our bodies.*

# Third group: tantalum

| | |
|---|---|
| 181<br>**Ta**<br>tantalum<br>73 | **tantalum**<br>*symbol: Ta • atomic number: 73 • period 6* |

Tantalum is a hard metal with a grey tinge. It slowly reacts with oxygen in the air to produce a thin layer of tantalum oxide, which protects the metal beneath from reacting any further. As a result, tantalum does not react with air, water or dilute acids, although it will react with concentrated sulphuric acid.

**Who discovered it?**  Tantalum was discovered in 1802 by the Swedish chemist, Anders Ekeberg. He isolated a new metal oxide from two **minerals**, but he could not isolate the free metal. However, Ekeberg was confident that he had discovered a new **element**, and he called it tantalum, after a mythical Greek king called Tantalus. This was because in Greek mythology the gods punished Tantalus by surrounding him with food and water that forever stayed just out of his reach, just as Ekeberg's new metal was out of his reach. Pure tantalum was finally isolated in 1903 by a German chemist called Werner von Bolton.

**Where is it found?**  Tantalum is only rarely found naturally as the free metal, and it makes up just 0.0002 per cent of the Earth's crust. The main **ore** of tantalum is tantalite, and about 1000 tonnes of tantalum are mined each year, mostly in Australia and Brazil. Tantalum is also found in the wastes from tin production. The ore is processed to concentrate the tantalum compounds, which are then converted to tantalum(V) fluoride, $TaF^5$, and heated with sodium to produce tantalum powder.

*This is a piece of tantalum ore. ▶*
*The crystals are made from*
*manganotantalite, a compound of*
*manganese, tantalum and oxygen.*

▲ *Tantalum capacitors are widely used to give the batteries in cellphones a boost when needed.*

**What are its main uses?** Tantalum has a very high melting point, the fourth highest of all the metals, so it was used to make the filaments for electric light bulbs at the start of the last century. Unfortunately, tantalum filaments were **brittle** and expensive. Once tungsten could be extracted cheaply, it took over from tantalum very quickly because it has the highest melting point of the metals.

## A tantalizing element

When tantalum is mixed with other metals, such as iron and nickel, it produces strong 'superalloys' that keep their strength at high temperatures and do not corrode easily. These contain up to 12 per cent tantalum, and are used in furnaces, heat shields and jet engines. As tantalum is unreactive, it does not react with blood and other body tissues, so it is used in medicine to make clips to seal blood vessels during surgery, and pins and plates to join shattered bones.

The biggest single use for tantalum, which uses about 60 per cent of the metal, is to make **capacitors**. These are electrical devices that store charge, and are widely used in cellphones, computers and electronics in cars. Without tantalum capacitors to give the battery a boost when needed, cellphones would be very much larger than they are.

# Fourth group: chromium

| 52 | | **chromium** |
|---|---|---|
| **Cr** | | *symbol: Cr • atomic number: 24 • period 4* |
| chromium | | |
| 24 | | |

Chromium is a shiny grey metal that is hard but **brittle**. It will react with hydrochloric acid and sulphuric acid, but it is usually protected from reacting with acids, air and water by a thin layer of chromium oxide that forms on its surface. Nitric acid actually helps this layer to form when it reacts with chromium. Chromium is not poisonous, but many of its **compounds** are, so they have to be handled with care.

*Who discovered it?*   Louis Vauquelin, a French chemist, discovered chromium in 1797 after studying a bright orange **mineral** called crocoite. Chemists knew that it contained lead, but Vauquelin suspected that it contained another metal. He managed to separate the lead from the rest of the mineral leaving a green solid, which was chromium oxide. Vauquelin isolated chromium metal the following year by heating the chromium oxide with powdered charcoal. He named the new metal after the Greek word for colour, because of all the different coloured solutions and solids he came across while trying to isolate chromium. Vauquelin discovered beryllium in the same year by studying emeralds, which are green because they contain small amounts of chromium.

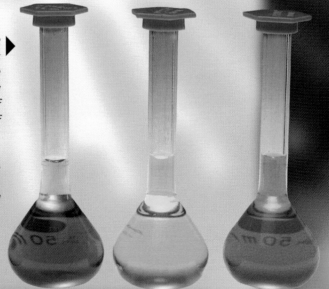

*Solutions of some common salts of chromium. The different colours show the complex nature of the chemistry of chromium metal. Chromium nitrate, $Cr(NO_3)_3$, is green while potassium chromate, $K_2CrO_4$, is yellow and potassium dichromate, $K_2Cr_2O_7$, is orange.*

◀ *This classic car has lots of shiny chromium plating to protect it from rusting.*

**Where is it found?** Chromium is not found naturally as the free metal, and it makes up just 0.014 per cent of the Earth's crust. Chromite (iron chromium oxide) is the main **ore** of chromium, and over 12 million tonnes of it are mined each year, mainly in South Africa, India and Kazakhstan. The ore is processed to form chromium oxide, which is then heated with aluminium to produce chromium.

*The word equation for the production of chromium is:*

chromium + aluminium → chromium + aluminium
    oxide                                       oxide

*This reaction happens because aluminium is more reactive than chromium.*

**What are its main uses?** The chromite ores themselves are useful, and only 20,000 tonnes of chromium metal are **extracted** from the millions of tonnes of chromite mined each year. The main use of chromium is in making **alloys** with iron.

## Stainless steel

Stainless steel contains between 12 per cent and 18 per cent chromium, and does not rust. The chromium reacts with oxygen in the air to form a protective layer of chromium oxide, which is too thin to be seen. If the steel is scratched, the freshly exposed chromium reacts with oxygen to repair the protective layer.

## Chrome plate

Chromium is also produced by **electrolysis** of solutions of chromium salts. This method is also used in 'chrome plating', where metal objects such as the bumpers of classic cars are plated with shiny chromium metal.

# Chromium compounds

Chromite, the main **ore** of chromium, has a very high melting point. Sand made from crushed chromite is used to make moulds for casting objects using molten metals. It is also used on its own or mixed with magnesium oxide to make heat-resistant refractory bricks for lining furnaces. Chromite can be processed to make other chromium compounds that are useful to us.

## Pigments, paints and precious stones

Lead chromate is used to make a range of **pigments**, used in paints and printing inks, that vary from light yellow to orange-red. Chromium oxide, $Cr_2O_3$, makes chrome green, a pigment that is used to colour cement, rubber and tiles. Chromium oxide also makes viridian, a dark green pigment used in paints for cars. Other chromium **compounds**, such as zinc chromate and calcium chromate, are used in paints to prime metals against rusting. Chromium oxide is added to glass by manufacturers to produce green glass. Chromium produces different colours in gemstones, depending on the arrangement of the different **atoms** around it in the crystal. Beryl is a colourless crystal made from a compound called beryllium aluminium silicate. However, if the beryl contains small amounts of chromium it becomes emerald, a beautiful green gemstone. Rubies are valuable gemstones consisting of corundum, which is aluminium oxide. Pure corundum is colourless, but rubies contain tiny amounts of chromium that give them an attractive deep red colour.

*Corundum produces colourless gems but with traces of chromium in the mineral it produces deep red rubies.* ▶

*Although leather itself is not poisonous, some people are allergic to the dichromates used to tan it, and they may suffer from a rash when they wear or carry leather items, such as this baseball mitt.*

## Tanning hide

Leather is made by treating raw animal skins with chemicals. This is called tanning, and without it the skins would become hard and rather smelly! The Romans tanned leather by soaking the skins in extracts from tree bark, but modern tanners use chromium salts such as potassium dichromate and ammonium dichromate. These chemicals are poisonous and may cause cancer, so workers in the tanneries need to take special care when they handle them.

## Dyes and cleaning

Sir William Perkin made the very first **artificial** dye in 1856 when he was only eighteen! He reacted a chemical from coal tar called phenylamine with potassium dichromate, and made a purple dye that he called aniline purple or 'mauve'. Various dichromates are still used to make textile dyes, and chromium hydroxide is used as a **mordant**, which is a chemical that helps dyes stick to the fibres in the cloth.

Chemists may clean their laboratory glassware using a strong acid called chromic acid. This is made by carefully reacting potassium dichromate with sulphuric acid. So much heat is produced in this **reaction**, that the container must be kept chilled using ice until the reaction is over. Chemists wear gloves and eye protection when handling chromic acid.

# Fourth group: molybdenum

| 96 Mo molybdenum 42 |
|---|

**molybdenum**
*symbol: Mo • atomic number: 42 • period 5*

Molybdenum is a very hard, silvery-white metal. It only reacts with air and oxygen when it is strongly heated, and it will not react with water, cold acids or alkalis, but it will react with hot sulphuric acid. Molybdenum has many uses, including making very strong steel, lamp filaments, electronic devices and heat shields. Molybdenum **compounds** are used as **catalysts** and lubricants.

*Who discovered it?*   Until the 18th century, almost any soft black **mineral** such as graphite or galena (lead sulphide) was called molybdenum, from the Greek word meaning lead. This changed after 1778 when the Swedish chemist Carl Scheele studied a mineral called molybdenite. He found that it reacted with chemicals in a very different way to graphite or galena. Scheele discovered that molybdenite reacted with nitric acid to produce a white solid, which we now know was molybdenum oxide. Although Scheele discovered and named molybdenum, it was his friend Peter Hjelm who managed to isolate it three years later. Hjelm heated the white molybdenum oxide with charcoal to produce molybdenum metal.

▼ *Transparent crystals of the mineral wulfenite, also known as yellow lead ore. It consists of lead molybdate, $PbMoO_4$, and is a minor source of molybdenum.*

The word equation for Hjelm's reaction to isolate molybdenum from molybdenum oxide is:

$$\text{molybdenum oxide} + \text{carbon} \rightarrow \text{molybdenum} + \text{carbon dioxide}$$

The **reaction** happens because the carbon in the charcoal is more reactive than molybdenum, so it is able to reduce the molybdenum oxide by removing the oxygen from it.

**Where is it found?** Molybdenum is not found naturally as the free metal, and it makes up just 0.0001 per cent of the Earth's crust. The main **ore** is molybdenite (molybdenum disulphide), the mineral that Scheele studied in the 18th century. The USA, Chile and China are the major producers of molybdenite, and over 130,000 tonnes of molybdenum is extracted in the world each year. The molybdenite ore is crushed, and then heated with air in a furnace to produce molybdenum oxide.

The word equation for the production of molybdenum oxide from molybdenite is:

$$\text{molybdenum disulphide} + \text{oxygen} \rightarrow \text{molybdenum oxide} + \text{sulphur dioxide}$$

Sulphur dioxide is an acidic gas, and care must be taken to make sure that it does not escape into the environment where it could cause acid rain.

The molybdenum oxide is purified further by distillation. It is heated to more than 1000 °C to turn it into a gas, which is cooled to produce very pure molybdenum oxide. This can be used to make other molybdenum compounds, or to make molybdenum metal by heating it strongly with hydrogen gas.

The word equation for the production of molybdenum from molybdenum oxide is:

$$\text{molybdenum oxide} + \text{hydrogen} \rightarrow \text{molybdenum} + \text{water}$$

The reaction happens because hydrogen is more reactive than molybdenum.

# Uses of molybdenum

Molybdenum has a high melting point and it keeps its strength at high temperatures. These are useful properties, and there are many tough jobs that molybdenum could do, except that it reacts with oxygen to produce molybdenum oxide when it gets hot. This means molybdenum itself is often used just for special jobs, such as rocket components, because these are only used once.

## Alloys

The biggest single use of molybdenum is in strong steel **alloys**, such as chrome molybdenum steel. This contains about 1 per cent chromium and about 0.25 per cent molybdenum. This small amount of molybdenum is enough to increase the strength of the steel, especially at high temperatures, and makes it less likely to wear down. Chrome molybdenum steel is used in aircraft, cars, machine tools (the equipment used to shape other metals in factories) and kitchen knives.

## Filaments and furnaces

The wire filaments in electric light bulbs are made from tungsten. The tungsten wire is coiled at the light bulb factory by wrapping it tightly around a molybdenum wire 'mandrel', a bit like wrapping a piece of string around a pencil. The molybdenum mandrel is removed by dissolving it in acid, leaving the coiled tungsten filament behind.

Molybdenum is a good conductor of electricity, so it is used to make the **electrodes** for electric furnaces. These are used in the manufacture of ceramics for electronic devices, and to melt glass. The molten glass surrounds the molybdenum electrodes and protects them from reacting with oxygen in the air.

## A slippery customer

When metal parts in machinery move past each other, a lot of friction is created. This makes it difficult for machinery to move easily. The moving parts wear away and the heat produced can even jam them together. Lubricants form a

▲ *Molybdenum disulphide is used to lubricate racing car engines. It sticks strongly to the metal surfaces in the engine but slides over itself easily. This lubricates the moving parts, and works even under extreme pressures and temperatures.*

slippery layer between the moving parts and reduce these problems. Graphite makes a good lubricant because it has layers that slide easily over one another (difficult zips can often be made to work smoothly by running a pencil over them). Molybdenum disulphide is a solid that is a very good lubricant, even at high temperatures. Just like the graphite from a pencil, layers of molybdenum disulphide slide easily over each other, reducing the friction between the moving surfaces.

## Oil refining

The different fractions or parts of crude oil are separated from each other by fractional distillation at oil refineries, but further chemical treatments are often needed before the products can be sold. Crude oil contains varying amounts of sulphur, which causes acid rain when fuels such as petrol and diesel are burnt. Molybdenum disulphide, cobalt–molybdenum and nickel–molybdenum **catalysts** help to remove the sulphur from the fuels, and so reduce the damage caused to the environment by acid rain.

# Fourth group: tungsten

| 184 | W | tungsten |
| --- | --- | --- |
| | tungsten | |
| 74 | | |

**tungsten**
*symbol: W • atomic number: 74 • period 6*

Tungsten is a strong, light-grey metal with the highest melting point of any of the metals. Powdered tungsten will react with the oxygen in the air, but larger pieces need to be heated very strongly before they react to produce tungsten oxide. Tungsten does not react with water or acids.

**Who discovered it?**  Tungsten was discovered and isolated by two Spanish chemists in 1783. Fausto d'Elhuyar and his older brother Juan José d'Elhuyar prepared an acid from a **mineral** called

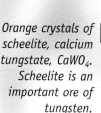

*Orange crystals of scheelite, calcium tungstate, $CaWO_4$. Scheelite is an important ore of tungsten.*

wolframite. Tungsten metal was produced when they strongly heated this acid with charcoal.
They called the new metal wolfram after the name of the mineral, and that is where the symbol for tungsten comes from. The name wolframite itself comes from German words meaning 'wolf dirt', because it was often found with tin **ore** and left a dirty impurity behind when the tin was **extracted**.

The Swedish chemist Carl Scheele had studied another ore containing tungsten two years before the d'Elhuyar brothers isolated tungsten. This ore was originally called tungsten itself, after the Swedish words meaning 'heavy stone', but was later named scheelite after the Swede. In English-speaking countries the metal is called tungsten, but elsewhere it is usually called wolfram.

**Where is it found?**  Tungsten makes up about 0.0001 per cent of the Earth's crust. Scheelite and wolframite are the main tungsten ores, and it is not found naturally as the free metal. These ores are found almost everywhere in the world, but China is the main producer. It supplies over 80 per cent of the world's needs, and Russia supplies most of the rest. About 45,000 tonnes of tungsten are extracted in the world each year, and a high percentage is recycled.

The extraction of tungsten from its ores is very complex and needs several stages. The ore is eventually converted to tungsten(VI) oxide, $WO_2$. This is heated with hydrogen or carbon at up to 1000 °C to convert it to tungsten powder. Bars of tungsten metal are produced by squashing the tungsten powder together and heating it for several hours.

The word equation for the production of tungsten from tungsten(IV) oxide using carbon is:

tungsten(IV) oxide + carbon → tungsten + carbon dioxide

## Tungsten carbide

Tungsten carbide, WC is a **compound** of tungsten and carbon. It is produced by reacting the two **elements** together at about 1500 °C. Carbides are often undesirable impurities formed when metals are extracted using carbon, but tungsten carbide is very useful. It is very hard and strong, and more rigid than steel. Tungsten carbide is widely used in drilling and cutting tools, including tools for cutting **ceramic** tiles, drilling glass and mining coal. It is up to one hundred times better at resisting wear than steel, and is used in various machine parts including snow ploughs and conveyor belts. It is also used for ballpoint pen tips.

◀ This miner is using a special type of drill that incorporates tungsten carbide, which makes it especially strong.

# Uses of tungsten

Tungsten is used instead of lead in environmentally-friendly fishing weights because it is denser than lead, but not poisonous like lead. It is also used to add weight to golf club heads and darts, and in armour-piercing anti-tank weapons. Tungsten has the highest melting point of all the metals, so it has a large number of important uses.

## Electric light bulbs

Ordinary household electric light bulbs, called incandescent lamps, contain a filament made from fine tungsten wire. When electricity is passed through the filament, it heats up and glows brightly. Tungsten is ideal because its high melting point means that the filament can get very hot, and produce more light, without melting. Tungsten is **brittle** and before scientists discovered how to make tungsten wire at the beginning of the last century, other metals such as platinum, osmium and tantalum had been tried. However, platinum has a much lower melting point than tungsten, while osmium and tantalum are more expensive. Also osmium filaments break too easily. Tungsten is used in many different types of incandescent lamp, including household bulbs, floodlights and car bulbs.

## Tungsten alloys

Tungsten is added to steel to improve its hardness and resistance to **corrosion** at high temperatures. Steel containing up to 6 per cent tungsten is used in car engine valves where it is exposed to corrosive gases and gets very hot. Tungsten is mixed with nickel and other metals to make 'superalloys' used in the aircraft industry, and it is an important ingredient with cobalt and chromium in very tough **alloys** used for bearings and pistons.

*Light bulbs produce light from a tungsten filament, which glows as it is heated by the electric current flowing through it.* ▶

*Some car rear-view mirrors contain a layer of electrochromic material containing tungsten(VI) oxide. This reduces the glare of any car headlights behind and makes it easier for the driver to see properly.*

## Light fantastic

Tungsten(VI) oxide is a yellow-white solid used to make bright yellow glazes for enamels and ceramics. If some of the oxygen **atoms** are removed, it becomes blue tungsten oxide, which is then easily converted back into tungsten(VI) oxide. This **reaction** is at the heart of window glass that can be darkened, and then lightened again, using electricity. Windows made from this glass are called electrochromic windows or Smart Windows. This new technology promises to save energy in the future because the amount of heat and light passing through them can be controlled easily.

## Electric tungsten

Silver is the best conductor of electricity and copper is nearly as good. Tungsten conducts electricity less than a third as well as these metals. However, unlike silver and copper it does not evaporate easily if a high current passes through it and, of course, it has a much higher melting point. This makes tungsten very useful for electrical heating coils in furnaces, cathode ray tubes (found in television sets and computer monitors), X-ray tubes and the magnetrons that produce microwaves in microwave ovens. Tungsten is used to make electrical contacts, although switches for very high voltage lines are made from tungsten–silver alloys or tungsten–copper alloys.

# Fifth group: manganese

| 55 | |
|---|---|
| **Mn** | **manganese** |
| manganese | symbol: Mn • atomic number: 25 • period 4 |
| 25 | |

Manganese is a shiny grey-white metal. It is next to iron in the **periodic table**, and it is similar to iron in its chemical **reactions**, but it is more hard and **brittle**. Manganese reacts only slowly with oxygen in the air, but it burns in air and oxygen when it is heated. Just like iron, it reacts very slowly with water at room temperature and it will rust in damp air. It reacts with dilute acids to produce manganese salts and hydrogen.

*Who discovered it?*   The Swedish chemist, Carl Scheele, discovered manganese in 1774 after an investigation lasting three years. He studied a black **mineral** called pyrolusite, which is manganese dioxide, and found that it produced a choking yellow-green gas when added to hydrochloric acid. Scheele realized that he had discovered a new metallic **element**, and a fellow Swede called Johann Gahn isolated manganese by heating pyrolusite with charcoal later that year. Scheele had in fact discovered chlorine gas at the same time, but he did not realize that it was a new element!

*Where is it found?*   Manganese is not found naturally as the free metal, but minerals containing manganese compounds are very common, and it makes up 0.1 per cent of the Earth's crust. Pyrolusite is the main **ore** of manganese, but other ores such as romanechite (barium manganese oxide) are also used. Over 7 million tonnes of

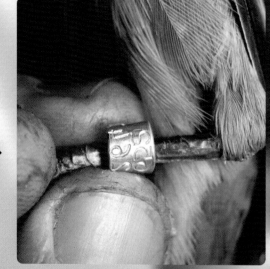

*Biologists often put rings on the legs of* ▶
*birds to help track them and monitor bird populations in different parts of the world. Tags of pure aluminium are too soft and easily corroded, and the birds may peck them off, so aluminium containing manganese is used instead.*

▲ *This ship's propellers are made from cast manganese bronze alloy. The manganese gives added strength and resists corrosion.*

manganese ore are mined each year, mainly in South Africa, Brazil and Ukraine. The ore is first processed to form manganese dioxide, which is then heated with aluminium and carbon to produce manganese.

**What are its main uses?**   Manganese is often added to other metals to improve their properties. Aluminium alloyed with small amounts of manganese is stronger and more resistant to **corrosion** than aluminium on its own. Copper, zinc and manganese make a very strong **alloy** called manganese bronze, which is used for hydraulic cylinders, valves and gears.

## Manganese in alloys

However, over 95 per cent of the manganese produced in the world each year is used in steel making, but without actually bothering to extract it first! Iron ore and manganese ore are processed together in electric furnaces to make an alloy of iron and manganese called ferromanganese, which is then used to make steel. Most steel contains up to 1 per cent manganese, which allows it to be rolled at high temperature without breaking.

# Manganese compounds

When the transition metals react with non-metals, such as oxygen, their **atoms** lose **electrons** to form particles called **ions**. Transition metals are unusual because they can form more than one type of ion, allowing lots of different **compounds** to be made. For example, manganese and oxygen react together to make manganese oxide, but there are three forms of it, and chemists use roman numbers to tell them apart. So, MnO is manganese(II) oxide, $Mn_2O_3$ is manganese(III) oxide and $MnO_2$ is manganese(IV) oxide. Potassium manganate(VII) is purple and has the formula $KMnO_4$, but potassium manganate(VI) has the formula $K_2MnO_4$ and is green! It might sound complicated, but it helps chemists keep track of the different compounds made by transition metals.

## Fertilizer, fungicides and food

Plants need manganese to grow properly, and their leaves turn yellow if they do not absorb enough. Some fertilizers contain manganese(II) sulphate, $MnSO_4$, to provide the soil with enough manganese for plants to grow properly. However, another manganese compound is used as a fungicide to kill fungi that cause diseases in crop plants. Manganese ethylene(bis)dithiocarbamate, more conveniently called 'Maneb', treats fruit and vegetables and stops mildew and other fungi spoiling the crop.

*One of these lettuces has been damaged by a fungal disease. A manganese compound is used to kill fungi that damage crop plants.*

We need manganese for our bones to develop properly. A normal diet should provide us with enough manganese, and cereals are a good source of the mineral. Manganese(II) chloride, $MnCl_2$, may be added to animal foods to avoid manganese deficiency in cattle and other animals. However, too much manganese can be dangerous. Manganese miners or steel workers exposed to manganese dust can develop manganism, a disease that makes it difficult for them to control their muscles. As a result, care is taken to avoid exposure to manganese in industries where it is used.

## Amethysts and glass

Amethyst is an attractive purple semi-precious stone made from quartz. This is mostly silicon dioxide, but on its own it would be colourless. Small amounts of manganese and iron compounds in the quartz crystal alter the way that light is absorbed by the crystal, giving it a purple colour. Manganese compounds may be added deliberately to ordinary glass by glass manufacturers to produce glass with a purple tint. The name amethyst comes from Greek words meaning 'not drunk'. This is because people used to believe that amethyst, and drinking glasses coloured with manganese, allowed them to drink a lot of alcohol without getting drunk!

▼ Amethysts are purple because they contain small amounts of manganese.

# More manganese compounds

## Potassium manganate(VII)

Potassium manganate(VII) is a purple solid that is often called potassium permanganate.

It dissolves easily in water to produce a purple solution that can be used as a disinfectant. Fish keepers sometimes add potassium permanganate to their fish ponds to kill harmful bacteria, parasites and fungi that may be infecting the fish. The right dose turns the water a very pale pink colour, but too much can kill the fish, so it must be used with care.

*The intense colour* ▲ *of potassium manganate(VII) is often used to show convection currents in water.*

Potassium manganate(VII) is a powerful **oxidizing agent**, which means that it can add oxygen to other chemicals or remove hydrogen from them. It is used to treat drinking water to control unpleasant smells and tastes, as it can react with many substances that cause these problems. Chemists use potassium manganate(VII) to make chlorine gas in the laboratory for their experiments. When it is added to concentrated hydrochloric acid, the acid starts to bubble and yellow-green chlorine gas is produced.

*The word equation for making chlorine gas in the laboratory is:*

potassium manganate(VII)
+
hydrochloric acid
→ manganese(II) chloride + potassium chloride + water + chlorine

## Manganese(IV) oxide

Over 200,000 tonnes of black manganese(IV) oxide (manganese dioxide) are used in the world each year. Although it can be made from other manganese **compounds**, it occurs naturally as pyrolusite (the main **ore** of manganese). Glass often contains iron impurities that give it a faint green tint. Glass manufacturers often add powdered manganese(IV) oxide to their glass to react with the iron compounds and remove the green tints.

Manganese(IV) oxide is a useful **catalyst**. In school laboratories it may be used to show the action of a catalyst on hydrogen peroxide solution. Hydrogen peroxide, $H_2O_2$, breaks down very slowly to form water and oxygen. However, if even a small amount of manganese(IV) oxide is added, it rapidly breaks down, producing lots of bubbles of oxygen very rapidly.

In industry, manganese(IV) oxide is used as a catalyst in the production of **artificial** flavourings. It is also used in batteries as a 'depolariser'. Hydrogen gas is produced inside batteries as they work, which would stop the electricity flowing. The depolariser oxidizes the hydrogen to water and keeps the battery working. Manganese(IV) oxide is also used to make the negative **electrodes** in alkaline batteries.

▼ *Alkaline batteries contain cathodes made from manganese dioxide.*

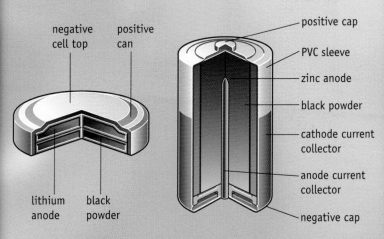

negative cell top

positive can

positive cap

PVC sleeve

zinc anode

black powder

cathode current collector

anode current collector

lithium anode

black powder

negative cap

# Fifth group: technetium

| 98 | Tc | technetium |
|---|---|---|
| | technetium | symbol: Tc • atomic number: 43 • period 5 |
| 43 | | |

Technetium is a silvery-grey metal that reacts in a similar way to rhenium, which is just below it in the **periodic table**. It does not react with air or water, but it reacts with oxygen when heated to produce technetium oxide. Technetium reacts with concentrated sulphuric acid and nitric acid, although it will not react with hydrochloric acid.

*Who discovered it?*   The 19th century was a busy time for chemists, with lots of new **elements** being discovered. When Dimitri Mendeleev published his periodic table in 1871, he realized that some elements might still be waiting to be found. He left gaps for them, including one for element number 43. In 1925, three German scientists, Ida Tacke, Walter Noddack and Otto Berg, were carrying out experiments on columbite ore. They announced the discovery of rhenium (see page 56) but also said they had found element 43. They called this element masurium, but other scientists doubted that they had really found it.

In 1937, two Italian scientists, Emilio Segrè and Carlo Perrier, isolated element 43 from a sample of molybdenum that had been bombarded with high-speed hydrogen **ions** in a machine called a particle accelerator. They called the new element technetium, from the Greek word for **artificial**. However, tiny amounts of technetium do occur naturally.

## Making technetium

There are more than 20 technetium isotopes, and they are all **radioactive**. Most of them **decay** very quickly into other elements, but the longest-lived isotope, technetium-98, has a **half-life** of over 4 million years. When uranium atoms decay, they can split to form technetium atoms, and tiny amounts of technetium are found in uranium **ore** as a result. Ida Tacke and her colleagues used columbite that contained some uranium, so it is possible that they were correct about masurium after all!

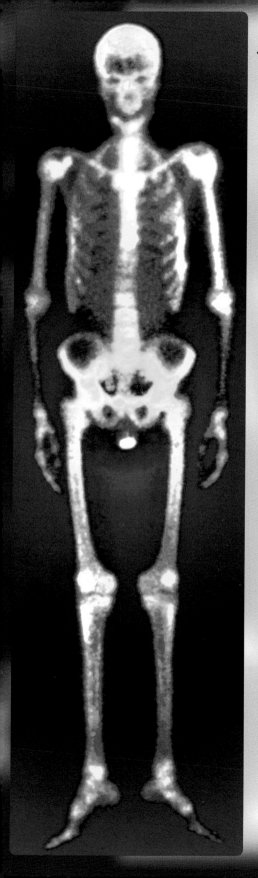

This is a bone scan of a healthy human skeleton, made using technetium-99 attached to a chemical called MDP (methylene diphosphonate) which concentrates in bones. A small amount is injected into the patient. A few hours later any damaged or infected areas of bone would show up as dark areas on the scan.

There is far too little technetium in uranium ore to be of any real use, but technetium-99 is produced by the kilogram from nuclear waste.

What are its main uses? Steel rusts when it is exposed to water and air, but not if a little potassium technetiate or ammonium technetiate is dissolved in the water. Steel can only be protected this way in special situations, such as in nuclear reactors, because technetium is radioactive. However, technetium and its **radiation** are very useful in nuclear medicine.

## Nuclear medicine

Doctors use technetium **compounds** to scan their patients for various diseases. Technetium-99 is used in more than 50 per cent of medical scans involving radioisotopes. It produces low-energy gamma rays that are easily detected. Its half-life is six hours, just long enough to examine the body but not so long that the patient gets a high dose of radiation. Different technetium compounds go to different parts of the body after being injected. This means that doctors can use different compounds to scan the skeleton, thyroid gland and organs such as the heart, brain and liver.

# Fifth group: rhenium

| 186 Re rhenium 75 | rhenium |
|---|---|
| | *symbol: Re • atomic number: 75 • period 6* |

Rhenium is a very dense, silvery metal with a high melting point. It does not react with air or water, but it reacts with oxygen when heated to produce rhenium oxide. Rhenium reacts with concentrated sulphuric acid and nitric acid, although it will not react with hydrochloric acid.

**Who discovered it?**   When Dimitri Mendeleev published his **periodic table** in 1871, he realized that there may be some undiscovered **elements**. So, he left gaps for them, including one for element number 75.

In 1925, three German scientists, Ida Tacke, Walter Noddack and Otto Berg, announced that they had discovered element number 75 in columbite **ore**. They called the missing element rhenium, after the Latin word for the River Rhine. Rhenium was the last naturally occurring element to be discovered – all other elements discovered since have been made **artificially**. A year later, Tacke managed to isolate rhenium; she also married her colleague Noddack!

**Where is it found?**   Rhenium makes up a tiny proportion of the Earth's crust, and on average there is less than a gram of it in every 400 tonnes of rock. It is not found naturally as the free element or in any particular **mineral**, and most rhenium is produced as a by-product of **extracting** copper from its ores, particularly those from the USA, Peru and Chile.

When the copper is refined, molybdenum and rhenium are left over in the waste material. The rhenium is separated from the molybdenum, concentrated and converted into ammonium perrhenate (pronounced 'pur-reenate'), which is then processed to make other **compounds** and rhenium metal. Fewer than 30 tonnes of rhenium are produced in the world each year.

**What are its main uses?** Rhenium is used as a **catalyst**, particularly by the oil industry to produce unleaded petrol. However, the main use for rhenium, which uses about 70 per cent of the metal, is in **alloys** with other metals.

## Spacecraft and filaments

When rhenium is added to molybdenum and tungsten, they become easier to work and can be **welded** without becoming **brittle**. Molybdenum containing up to 50 per cent rhenium is used in aircraft and spacecraft, and tungsten containing up to 25 per cent rhenium is used to make the filaments for electric lamps. Rhenium has the second highest melting point of all the metals, and it keeps its strength even when it has been heated and cooled lots of times, so it is used in the thrusters that keep satellites in the correct position.

▼ *Crude oil is processed at oil refineries, like this one, to produce petrol, diesel and other important substances. Rhenium is the catalyst used to produce unleaded petrol.*

## Elements

The table below contains some information about the properties of the transition metals in this book. The artificial **elements**, rutherfordium, dubnium, seaborgium and bohrium are not included because very little is known about them.

| Element | Symbol | Atomic number | Melting point (°C) | Boiling point (°C) | Density (g/cm³) |
|---|---|---|---|---|---|
| chromium | Cr | 24 | 1903 | 2672 | 7.2 |
| hafnium | Hf | 72 | 2230 | 5197 | 13.3 |
| manganese | Mn | 25 | 1245 | 1962 | 7.4 |
| molybdenum | Mo | 42 | 2617 | 4612 | 10.3 |
| niobium | Nb | 41 | 2468 | 4742 | 8.57 |
| rhenium | Re | 75 | 3180 | 5627 | 21.0 |
| scandium | Sc | 21 | 1541 | 2831 | 2.99 |
| tantalum | Ta | 73 | 2996 | 5425 | 16.6 |
| technetium | Tc | 43 | 2172 | 4877 | 11.5 |
| titanium | Ti | 22 | 1660 | 3287 | 4.5 |
| tungsten | W | 74 | 3407 | 5657 | 19.3 |
| vanadium | V | 23 | 1700 | 3380 | 6.1 |
| yttrium | Y | 39 | 1507 | 3338 | 4.47 |
| zirconium | Zr | 40 | 1852 | 4377 | 6.50 |

The following elements can be found in *The Transition Metals: Gold, Iron and Other Metals.*

| Element | Symbol | Element | Symbol |
|---|---|---|---|
| cadmium | Cd | osmium | Os |
| cobalt | Co | palladium | Pd |
| copper | Cu | platinum | Pt |
| gold | Au | rhodium | Rh |
| hassium | Hs | ruthenium | Ru |
| iridium | Ir | silver | Ag |
| iron | Fe | ununbium | Uub |
| meitnerium | Mt | darmstadtium | Ds |
| mercury | Hg | roentgenium | Rg |
| nickel | Ni | zinc | Zn |

# Compounds

These tables show you the chemical formulas of a selection of the **compounds** mentioned in the book. For example, chromic acid has the formula $H_2CrO_4$. This means it is made from two hydrogen **atoms**, one chromium atom and four oxygen atoms, joined together by chemical bonds.

**Chromium compounds**

| Chromium compounds | formula |
|---|---|
| calcium chromate | $CaCrO_4$ |
| chromic acid | $H_2CrO_4$ |
| chromium hydroxide | $Cr(OH)_3$ |
| chromium oxide | $Cr_2O_3$ |
| potassium dichromate | $K_2Cr_2O_7$ |

**Hafnium compounds**

| Hafnium compounds | formula |
|---|---|
| hafnium(IV) oxide | $HfO_2$ |
| hafnium carbide | $HfC$ |
| hafnium(IV) chloride | $HfCl_4$ |

**Manganese compounds**

| Manganese compounds | formula |
|---|---|
| manganese(II) chloride | $MnCl_2$ |
| manganese(II) oxide | $MnO$ |
| manganese(III) oxide | $Mn_2O_3$ |
| manganese(IV) oxide (manganese dioxide) | $MnO_2$ |
| manganese(II) sulphate | $MnSO_4$ |
| potassium manganate(VI) | $K_2MnO_4$ |
| potassium manganate(VII) (potassium permanganate) | $KMnO_4$ |

**Molybdenum compounds**

| Molybdenum compounds | formula |
|---|---|
| molybdenum disulphide | $MoS_2$ |
| molybdenum oxide | $MoO_3$ |

**Niobium compounds**

| Niobium compounds | formula |
|---|---|
| columbite (niobite) | $FeNb_2O_6$ |
| niobium(V) oxide | $Nb_2O_5$ |

**Scandium compounds**

| Scandium compounds | formula |
| --- | --- |
| scandium chloride | $ScCl_2$ |
| scandium fluoride | $ScF_2$ |

**Tantalum compounds**

| Tantalum compounds | formula |
| --- | --- |
| tantalum(V) fluoride | $TaF_5$ |
| tantalite | $FeTa_2O_6$ |

**Titanium compounds**

| Titanium compounds | formula |
| --- | --- |
| rutile | $TiO_2$ |
| titanium(IV) chloride | $TiCl_2$ |
| titanium(IV) oxide | $TiO_2$ |

**Tungsten compounds**

| Tungsten compounds | formula |
| --- | --- |
| tungsten carbide | $WC$ |
| tungsten(VI) oxide | $WO_3$ |

**Vanadium compounds**

| Vanadium compounds | formula |
| --- | --- |
| carnotite | $K_2(UO_2)_2(VO_4)_2$ |
| vanadium(V) oxide | $V_2O_5$ |

**Yttrium compounds**

| Yttrium compounds | formula |
| --- | --- |
| bastnasite | $Y(CO_3)F$ |
| gadolinite | $Y_2FeBe_2Si_2O_{10}$ |

**Zirconium compounds**

| Zirconium compounds | formula |
| --- | --- |
| baddelyite, zirconium(IV) oxide | $ZrO_2$ |
| zircon, zirconium silicate | $ZrSiO_4$ |

# Glossary

**alloy** mixture of two or more metals, or a mixture of a metal and a non-metal. Alloys are often more useful than the pure metal on its own.

**alpha radiation (α radiation)** radiation caused by quickly moving helium nuclei which have broken away from an unstable nucleus

**artificial** man-made

**atom** smallest particle of an element that has the properties of that element. Atoms contain smaller particles called subatomic particles.

**atomic number** number of protons in the nucleus of an atom. It is also called the proton number.

**brittle** the word that describes a solid that breaks into small pieces when hit. Glass is a brittle solid because it breaks into small pieces of glass when hit with a hammer.

**capacitor** electrical component that stores electric charge in a circuit

**catalyst** substance that speeds up a reaction without getting used up

**ceramic** tough solid made by heating clay and other substances to high temperatures in an oven. Plates, bathroom tiles and toilet bowls are made from ceramics.

**compound** substance made from the atoms of two or more elements, joined together by chemical bonds

**corrosion** when a substance forms on the surface of a metal. Usually this is an oxide of the metal produced when the metal reacts with oxygen in the air.

**decay** when the nucleus of a radioactive substance breaks up, giving off radiation and becoming the nucleus of another element, it decays

**density** mass of a substance compared to its volume. Substances with a high density feel very heavy for their size.

**electrode** solid that conducts electricity, such as graphite or a metal. Electrodes are found in batteries and are also used in electric furnaces, electrolysis and electroplating.

**electrolysis** breaking down or decomposing a compound by passing electricity through it. The compound must be molten or dissolved in a liquid for electrolysis to work.

**electron** sub-atomic particle with a negative electric charge. It is found around the nucleus of an atom.

**element** substance made from one type of atom. Elements cannot be broken down into simpler substances.

**extract** remove a chemical from a mixture of chemicals

**group** vertical column of elements in the periodic table. Elements in a group have similar properties.

**half-life** time taken for half the atoms of a radioactive substance to decay

**ion** charged particle made when atoms lose or gain electrons. If a metal atom loses electrons it becomes a positive ion. If a non-metal atom gains electrons it becomes a negative ion.

**isotope** atom of an element with the same number of protons and electrons, but different numbers of neutrons. It shares the same atomic number but has a different mass number.

**laser** stands for light amplification by stimulated emission of radiation. Laser light has special properties, including a small range of frequencies and spreading out very little.

**mass number** in the nucleus of an atom, the number of protons added to the number of neutrons

**mineral** substance that is found naturally but does not come from animals or plants. Metal ores and limestone are examples of minerals.

**mordant** chemical that helps a dye to stick to fabric fibres

**neutron** sub-atomic particle with no electric charge, found in the nucleus of an atom

**nucleus** part of an atom made from protons and neutrons. It has a positive electric charge and is found at the centre of the atom.

**ore** mineral from which metals can be taken out and purified

**oxidizing agent** substance that can oxidise other substances

**period** horizontal row of elements in the periodic table

**periodic table** table in which all the known elements are arranged into groups and periods

**phosphor** chemical that gives off light when it absorbs energy

**pigment** solid substance that gives colour to a paint. Pigments do not dissolve in water.

**proton** sub-atomic particle with a positive electric charge, found in the nucleus of an atom

**proton number** number of protons in the nucleus of an atom. It is also called the atomic number. No two elements have the same proton number.

**radioactive** substance that can produce radiation

**radiation** energy or particles given off when an atom decays

**reaction** chemical change that produce new substances

**refining** removing impurities from a substance to make it more pure. It can also mean separating the different substances in a mixture, for example, in oil refining.

**sub-atomic particle** particle smaller than an atom, such as proton, neutron and electron

**tracer** chemical, often radioactive, that scientists can easily follow to see where it goes

**weld** join two pieces of metals, usually by heating them

# Timeline

| | | |
|---|---|---|
| manganese and molybdenum discovered | 1774–1778 | Carl Scheele |
| tungsten discovered | 1783 | Fausto and Juan José d'Elhuyar |
| zirconium discovered | 1789 | Martin Klaproth |
| titanium discovered | 1791 | William Gregor |
| yttrium discovered | 1794 | Johan Gadolin |
| chromium discovered | 1797 | Louis Vauquelin |
| niobium and vanadium discovered | 1801 | Charles Hatchett; Andrés Manuel del Río |
| tantalum discovered | 1802 | Anders Ekeberg |
| scandium discovered | 1879 | Lars Nilson |
| hafnium discovered | 1923 | Dirk Coster and Georg von Hevesy |
| rhenium discovered | 1925 | Ida Tacke, Walter Noddack and Otto Berg |
| technetium isolated | 1937 | Emilio Segrè and Carlo Perrier |
| rutherfordium, dubnium, seaborgium and bohrium first made | 1964–1981 | Various institutes in Russia, USA and Germany |

# Further reading and useful websites

## Books

Fullick, Ann, *Science Topics: Chemicals in Action* (Heinemann Library, 1999)

Knapp, Brian, *The Elements* series, particularly, *Iron, Chromium and Manganese* (Atlantic Europe Publishing Co, 1996)

Oxlade, Chris, *Chemicals in Action* series, particularly *Metals; Atoms; Elements* and *Compounds* (Heinemann Library, 2002)

## Websites

WebElements™
http://www.webelements.com
An interactive periodic table crammed with information and photographs.

Proton Don
http://www.funbrain.com/periodic
The fun periodic table quiz!

DiscoverySchool
http://school.discovery.com/students
Help for science projects and homework, and free science clip art.

BBC Science
http://www.bbc.co.uk/science
Quizzes, news, information and games about all areas of science.

Creative Chemistry
http://www.creative-chemistry.org.uk
An interactive chemistry site with fun practical activities, quizzes, puzzles, etc.

Mineralogy Database
http://www.webmineral.com
Lots of useful information about minerals, including colour photographs and information about their chemistry.

# Index